SEPPUKU
QUARTERLY

SEPPUKU QUARTERLY

Seppuku Quarterly/Joseph Fulkerson
ISBN: 978-1-7371509-8-5
Laughing Ronin Press

www.LaughingRoninPress.com

sep·pu·ku /ˈsepo͞oˌko͞o, səˈpo͞oˌko͞o/

(Japanese: 切腹, "cutting [the] belly"), sometimes referred to as harakiri is a form of Japanese ritual suicide by disembowelment.

It was favoured under Bushidō (warrior code) as an effective way to demonstrate the courage, self-control, and strong resolve of the samurai and to prove sincerity of purpose.

Thanks to all who contributed to this issue, with a special thanks to Ron Whitehead, U.S. National Beat Poet Laureate

English Means Success

Kevin Tosca

Seeing Amsterdam's Gothic facades and Dutch gables surrounded by all that calm dark water made me feel something no city had ever made me feel before: Forgetful.

Blissfully so.

And what did these ornamental anorexic houses allow me to forget?

Man.

Man?

Yes, man. Not the ones who built this, the ones who now breathed this. My so-called contemporaries. Them and their repugnant manly presence.

Aren't you being harsh? A bit of a Jimmy Generalizer?

No.

But the forgetful magic didn't last forever. Didn't even last a day.

I remembered my fellow men—I mean the tourists—but I especially mean the English-spewing Hopalong Cassidy Rapists.

The dumb stench of marijuana in the air didn't help, nor did the vulgar reputation of the damn place or the impossible number of shiny happy people *on vacation*. It all did, however, give birth to an idea, and that idea was this:

Every English-infected man-goon and woman-goon I saw was high.

And I thought: Yes! Every last one of them *is* high! Rocky Mountain high! Stoned out of their gourds high! Welcome to the monkey house high!

That's it!

That's *got* to be it!

That's why this world is such a cruel and soul-crushing place. *That's* why man is such a benighted asinine animal.

Here, in Amsterdam, is his benighted asinine face.

Here, like in Las Vegas and Times Square and on the Champs Élysées, the FACE is on twenty-four-hour display.

Here, and always, even the good girls want to hooker gawk and brownie binge. They just wanna have fun.

Fun!

What a heinous, unforgivable idea.

So what if the Dutch go about their business, mind it and only it and cultivate their little gardens.

So what if they're a relatively healthy, happily godless people.

They are staggeringly outnumbered.

Even in their own country—even in this mesmerizing city of theirs—they are the enlightened minority, and they will pay the enlightened minority's price.

MARY MORRIS' TOE, TAP AND BALLET SCHOOL'S YEAR-END RECITAL, Far Rockaway, Long Island.

Jean Colonomos

I get my first big break when I'm five.

I'm a watering can.

I tiptoe around a circle of six girls,

also barely out of toddlerhood,

believing my arm is a spout.

I bend over each girl curled

on the floor and pour.

A little one rises on her knees,

opens her arms and   blooms.

During the finale, *Dance with the Dolly with the Hole in Her Stocking*, disaster strikes. Decked out in a sea of blue tulle tutus, wristbands and bows, we walk towards the audience shaking our wrists. Two bruisers on either side try to block me but my ego elbows away their dough-baby bodies. I dream of *Sleeping Beauty's* Aurora. And Odette, the Princess *Swan Lake's* sorcerer, Von Rothbart, has turned into a swan, keeps her and a corps de ballet of sixty women imprisoned in birds' bodies. I long to be the trapped white *cygne**, her rippling arms like wings, her gliding movements a sacrificial rite of passage.

Oh the miracle of
transcendence that makes you
other than who you are.

*cygne-swan, French

MIDNIGHT FUCKHEAD

Kevin Ridgeway

I wanted to kill the asshole
dressed like a tweaker variation
of Christian Slater's onscreen
impersonation of Jack Nicholson
behind sunglasses for telling me
not to deny I was playing under
the covers with my dick over
the knockers on the crazy girl
outside in the common area
of the local mental hospital. I
screamed and ran out of the room.
They moved me to a room with an
old man with dementia who burst into
tears as he looked out our window
and couldn't even remember the last
son of a bitch who pissed him off.

BROKEN LIGHT

Kevin Ridgeway

My girlfriend died drunk
in the same house as her,
and I'm afraid to talk to her
about it. I'm even told
she found her. I've kept
myself trapped deep
in the double-edged
sword of a heartbroken
midnight I thought I was
still too young to know.
My cigarette goes unlit
and I don't notice it while
she and I both stare at
one another behind
large sunglasses from
across the parking lot
during the routine patient
smoke break at the local
psych ward we're
both being treated at.
She's getting discharged

after winning a cheap
carnival game before
lunch. She hands me
the fun size chocolate
candy bars she's won,
which has sweetened
the unspoken darkness
still between us.

if I don't make it to the feast

Tanya Rakh

tell the muses

and their lovely ghosts

I tried—

no ghost can suffer

this lonely,

erratic trying

I tongue each bloodstain on

your darkest curtains,

always trying

to taste home

The email that finds you well

Josh Dale

is lost amongst 999+ other emails that have found you
with blurry incoherent eyes scanning and doomscrolling
and popping notification pills with your Zoloft and crummy
tap water. And then the ones that find you unwell are always
the ones you happen to skim across when you're already in
the gutter and unlike Oscar Wilde you're not looking up at the
stars but a blue-light rectangle containing anything and
everything turned to the highest brightness exactly 5'-9.5"
away from an airport outlet as you wait for the snow to calm
the fuck down and the tarmac to turn black again. It's time to
leave it all behind the email says to you buried under other
emails all hoping to find you well. And just like the snow burying
you and thousands of others it's time to leave it all behind.

Sunday Breakfast, Next Booth Over

Paul Cordeiro

Finishing their hotcakes
and scrambled
special with sausage,
the louder talker
in the next booth over
grins with braces.
I hear his static.
Both men wear pinstripes
like luxury car salesman.
But then capped front teeth
banters on about Brady's
longevity, how he met
him once on Federal Hill.
Both men overtip
and step out in cordovan brogues
bright as the dome of a city
aptly named Providence.

PREFACE

Roberta Gould

Nothing is lost
Shuffle it
And when you reach in
it's creation again!
You don't need much
just a little wonder
The cup in your hand
draws its own water
and will till the seas
run dry and the rain
fails to become a river
you at the end of an epoch
or a spark in celestial combustion
more than you bargained for
here where you happened to be born

"Kept Alive"

Drew Campbell

Scribbles of ink,

Smeared on tiles of foundation.

Words spoken,

To all senses at once.

Aboard the vessel,

Into the distance.

The spark is acknowledged,

But the message is incomplete.

A beginning,

To an unfolding.

Lives in question…

Unanswered fate…

Past the view of the scribe's gaze,

The consequences manifest.

A collection of unknowns.

Shimmering, possible outcomes.

Converging into storms.

The mind alive with alteration.

Breaths of reconstruction.

Toggling the fibers of being.

Taking on a new existence.

Separate from limitation.

A world ignited,

With fertile waters...

Getting Philosophical @ Nellies

Tim Heerdink

for Jon Koker

Sometimes, you just need someone
to say, *Fuck,*
let's go get some steak & eggs
& have ourselves
a little pity party
so we can get back to work.

We all find ourselves in the pit
some point along our journey;
it's up to you to decide
whether you're the lion
or the pile of bones
from a man who pissed himself
before succumbing to his fate.

Can I get you some more coffee?
the waitress asks as I'm switching hats,
trying to figure out which I am
in this pit we're in,
but yes,

with that butter
for the fat
this body needs
to keep this mind
on edge.

I hate to see a brother drown;
it reminds me of me yesterday,
& so the knives & forks clink
while the waitress lingers
wanting to overhear

all this talk of what we could be
if we just let ourselves
get out of our own way.

Old Beds

Dave Cullern

homesick

in vigorous streets of

paced

paving,

silent feet,

lights of adventures

play the space

above the signs

like a harp

like a lute

like a singer

with rags wrapped around lonely joints

and a voice marked by songs

now lost

in their ears

steps like

breaths like

beats like

flight like

flows of the rivers of roads

with no maps

to the pits

bolt the door

because we cried a long time ago

we don't cry any more

Love note from your Good Girl

Claire Richardson

I'm not ready for the bin

Let me live on the sole of your shoe

Pummel me raw through gravel

Coat me almost suffocated in the wettest

Of mud

Let me sleep at the foot of your bed

Kicking me through your bad dreams

Dead night shivers

That warm with the morning mattress

Still there, beneath me

Keep me plump on your leftovers in the dog's bowl, tell

me I'm a Good Girl

Use any part of me or my absolute whole

Just don't throw me away

Doctor No

Catfish McDaris

Huge waves on Lake Michigan. a week ago, saw this guy with seven little kids playing on the beach, way too close to the violent water, I wanted to go warn him, but got closer, if I had to something I would. Luckily three ladies came and got them all out of danger. I went south to a poetry slam where I dropped to my knees and started wolf howling at The Green Mill in Chicago, birthplace of the slam and an old Capone hangout. An old friend and his Thai wife came and we went out for supper, he drove his new Mercedes...$2160,000. We couldn't fit in it, so our ladies rode behind us. Jerry and parked his magic car and we went in our car. The Merc., has a hard top convertible, you push a button and it disappeared into the trunk. Time for a new James Bond.

My Only No-Hitter

Ron Whitehead

A no-hitter is as magical as a blue moon.
I was 12. My brother Brad was 10.

I was pitcher and Brad was catcher
for our Centertown Demons Little League

baseball team. Back in the early 1960s,
in small towns across Kentucky,

the baseball park was where
all the folks in and around farming

and mining communities gathered
to socialize and to play baseball and softball.

Ladies in the concession stands
cooked and sold hamburgers and hot dogs.

Gossip was shared, stories told,
moths of all sizes circled and often died

in the big bright lights of the hot summer nights.
That particular night we were playing Rockport

in the championship game
of a Little League Tournament.

Some of the small town teams had trouble
rounding up enough players in the 9 to 12 age

so it wasn't uncommon for them to add
older players to their rosters. Rockport had

27

3 or 4 older players. The oldest had to be 16.
He was huge and had a pretty good moustache.

Jackie Maddox was our coach. He was tough
but always positive. He drilled us over and over

on the basics of the game. Brad and I
had already learned all the basics from Daddy,

and our uncle Roy, but we got better playing
for Jackie. He added new tips and angles to

our games. We paid close attention to everything
he said. And he went by all the rules so all

our players met the Little League age requirements.
Brad and I played every day. Daddy taught us

how to play pepper, with and without gloves.
Daddy and Roy taught me how to throw breaking balls.

I worked hard to develop a curve and a sinker.
I worked on a knuckle ball, like my cousin Butch Ford,

who went on to pitch for Tennessee, but at 12
years of age my hand wasn't big enough to get

the grip I needed for a knuckler. Brad and I were both
students of the game. We studied, watched,

and played constantly. The stands were packed.
By the 4th inning people were standing and screaming

at and for every batter and with each play.
I had developed my control so I could throw the ball

to the exact spot where Brad placed his glove.
Brad, as catcher, gave me the hand signal for each pitch.

If I liked what Brad called I nodded Yes
and if I wanted to throw something different

I nodded No. I usually went with what Brad called.
He knew the game. It was a hard-fought battle

with both teams playing well, wanting to win.
After 6 innings the game was tied, 0 to 0.

Pitching and defense for both teams was excellent.
In the top of the 7th, and final, inning Neal Grant

led us off with a single to left field. I stepped up
to the plate and on the first pitch bunted the ball

right down the third base line. Neal made it to 2nd
and I made it safely to 1st. Then David Button

struck out. Brad batted cleanup. He drilled a single
to center field. Neal scored. I advanced to 3rd.

David Everly grounded to short stop. Rockport
turned a double play to end our at bat. But, for

the first time in the game, we had scored a run
and taken the 1 to nothing lead. The fans

were going crazy. Folks from Rockport and
Centertown were jumping up and down

and screaming. Daddy and a group of men
stood right behind the umpire. They were all

yelling real loud, coaching us. Our coach,
Jackie Maddox, gathered us in the dugout

and said, "Okay boys, stay calm. Remember
everything I've taught you. We've got this."

We all raised our hands high and touched
them together and screamed "GO TEAM!"

and ran back out onto the field for the bottom
of the 7th inning. I had somehow managed

to strike out 17 of the 18 batters I had faced
up until now. In the bottom of the 7th

I was facing the top of Rockport's lineup.
The first batter up hit a hot grounder

to Jackie Tomlinson at 3rd base. Jackie
scooped it up and made the long throw

to 1st. David Button leaned way out and,
nearly colliding with the runner, made

the catch. One out. I hit the corners on
the 2nd batter and the Rockport man

who was umpire behind the plate made,
in my eyes, some terrible calls. I went

to 3-2, full count, then walked the batter.
Runner on 1st. 3rd batter in the lineup

grounded my 1st pitch to 2nd base
where Steve Everly made a good catch

and tagged 2nd base, forcing out the runner.
2 down, 1 to go. And sure enough

Rockport's cleanup hitter was the 6 foot
2 inch moustached 16-year-old.

For my 1st pitch I threw a fastball
right at his crotch. He jumped back

and turned towards me, holding his bat up,
staring me down, warning me that I'd

better not do that again. I had developed
what appeared to be a straight over the top

fastball but it was my drop ball. When
the throw neared the plate the bottom

dropped out. Brad called drop ball.
The batter went for it. 1 strike, 1 ball.

For my next pitch Brad called a curve.
I had a curve that went 2 and occasionally

3 feet sideways and down. I pulled
everything out for this one. It curved

3 feet. He went for it and missed
by a mile. 2 strikes, 1 ball, 2 outs.

Bottom of the 7th. Every fan in the stands
and standing at the edges of the field

was either screaming their heads off
or standing open mouthed, breathless.

Brad called inside fast ball. I threw
the pitch inside down around the batter's

knees. He didn't go for it. 2 strikes, 2 balls.
He fouled off my next pitch. Then

I threw high and inside for ball 3. Full count.
I turned away from the plate, took a deep breath,

then turned back for Brad's call. I nodded Yes.
I launched what appeared, to the batter,

to be another fastball. But 2 feet in front
of the center of the plate, what appeared

to be the perfect pitch for the batter, the ball
dropped 2 feet, from navel to below knees.

The batter swung and wildly missed.
I struck him out. The place went nuts.

We won! 1 to 0. We won the championship.
Best game I ever pitched. My only no-hitter.

Left to right: my brother Brad Whitehead, cousin Bruce "Brucie" Patton, Uncle Steve "Stevie" Render, and yours truly Ron Whitehead, on our way to the game. Photo by Mama aka Greta Render Whitehead.

"Starve the Poets"

Tohm Bakelas

reading the translated
words of Yi Sha,
i can't stop myself from
thinking of things
i'd rather be doing

Starve the Poets, yes Mr. Sha,
I agree, but your book
starved me
of poetry.

"big hammer street value"

Tohm Bakelas

for dave roskos

i've mailed hundreds of letters
and poems to people
all over the world
but i've never pulled some

blaze foley shit and
used duct-tape
to seal the envelopes—
although i suppose i should
expect nothing less
living in
new jersey

Tumble dried memory and a penny in pocket
Steve Zmijewski

Misled

downhill

in a dried, thirty gal whiskey barrel.

Anyone can have a good time, though it depends on

the condition of being definite.

Rusted boots and forgetful

loops,

we don't want to be forgotten.

The spins thereafter reminded you of that cute brunette

who once

paid for your soda.

And the man at the counter, with the different color

glasses, confusedly spoke of needing

a proper, bigger bookcase.

Guessed he was waiting for an empty and blank face,

(like ours) built nice and willing to listen.

And he said,

we're all rushing to leave because the things we see

are no longer so lovely. I'll be glad

when I finally get away. I'm still young enough,

just a former shade of aspiring.

Some days the heat is too much. It's not

worth the water we boil.

Thought it'd be raining. Everything could use a rinse.

Oh, hey, here...

Better hold onto this penny.

Decorum

Aimee Nicole

When you see

these old habits

sneak in like

thieves dressed in jewels,

I need you to

wrap my hair

around your fist

and get a firm grip.

Hold my gaze

until I break.

I'm like a horse

that way.

I want to be

ridden so desperately

by you that

any command

is doctrine.

Our Gospel

Aimee Nicole

And I promise when
I fall out of love
it will be like
falling off
the highest cliff.
Quick plunge into
arctic waters
extinguishing every flame.
Every knick knack
will smolder and ash
to nothing but a bad dream.
We'll wake up and convince
ourselves those words we once
whispered under covers
in twilight were once true as Gospel.

Renting a VCR in 1989

John Dorsey

we didn't have our own
the only copy
of bill & ted's excellent adventure
was always out

& i was still too young
to alter the course of history

not yet lovesick
for pale girls
chanting nirvana anthems
drinking wine coolers
in the suburban garages
of my youth

sitting there indian style
with unsalted popcorn on a paper towel
on a green shag carpet
that never looked clean

no matter how many times
you tried to scrub the memories out

i spent my saturday nights
watching cronenberg
& hal hartley's
loveletters to long island outsiders
feeling just as weird & out of place
as i was supposed to
waiting on the future.

My Singularity

Kathleen Denizard

I

Toward the future, wisdom may look and see another being like me

Indelible as the past may seem, memory forgets the worn-out wheel that rolled us into invention

And kept going

Masterminds of the scientific are craftsmen in a novel age of extreme creation

Where evolution is genius in a petri dish that could take us back to ourselves

But if I am discovered in a biosphere beyond, will my heart and soul be there?

II

We would meet that day outside the lab complex

Between mid-morning sunlight that fired through a row of evergreens lining direction to the parking lot

Where experts of the DNA and masters of apery will bring a life renascent to my time

I take the appointed place among my comrades, nervously suspended in rising uncertainty

Running my fingers through my hair as is my habit

Pondering still the welcoming of genetic invasion

And then, as though seeing myself step out of a mirror, he approached

Staring, awe-struck, considering me as his twin stranger

I offered my hand to say, how do you do?

He did not return a shake, just lifted his hand to run his fingers through his hair.

Jacob Louis Beaney

free lunch

Bashō could
pay for lunch
with a poem

~

what can I get
in the supermarket
with this?

the cosmic worm

the room melted,
into a wave of a billion
colours

~

I turned into a worm,
and journeyed
the cosmos.

Joshua St. Claire

staccato lightning
the twitch twitch
of the junkie's fingers

pigeons take a shit
on the overpass
graffiti

The Roomer

Ed Ahern

Petey never talked to our therapy group about Holly, although he was even worse off after she happened to him. He'd been living alone, except for a scrawny cat, and the cat had just died.

A few years earlier, he'd been in a motorcycle accident. His right leg had been removed from the knee down, and his left leg was always in a shin high medical boot. He wasn't comfortable talking about his legs with our group, telling me privately that he felt their attention was hijacked by his triad of cane, metal leg and bright plastic boot.

"So the insurance company finally settled?" I asked.

He smiled wryly. "Yeah, George, between disability the insurance payout and eventually a half-assed pension, I can live a long, busted-up life."

Whenever he could he sat in a tall, upright chair. Standing up if he was too low to the ground was painful to watch and, judging by his expression, painful to attempt. Petey infrequently shaved and had let his hair grow long, but from the knees up he was a normally grungy-looking guy.

Holly was a major part of our group, grifting a little because she had to, but sympathetic to everyone's problems. She was an alumnus of a drug rehab, divorced, living in a shelter, kids with the dad. Her clothes were Catholic charity, but her few bits of jewelry looked expensive. "I hate the shelter," she'd tell us, "because half of us are using and I'm offered hits all the time, and because stuff gets stolen every day." I watched her head turn toward him while Petey began a rare sharing to us all.

"Okay, I've got enough to live comfortably, family house paid off, but it takes me over a half-hour to gather and put out the garbage, and an hour to undress, shower and dress again. I'm not bitching, some of us have it worse in different ways, but I remember what it was like to be better."

I sat near Petey, and scanned everyone's eyes. They were staring, not at Petey's face, but at his cripple's trinity. Except for Holly—she focused on Petey, broadcasting warmth. When the meeting ended, she cut across the circle of chairs to talk to him as he struggled to stand.

"Nobody here has experienced what it's like for

you. We're screwed up inside. You're torn up outside and in." She paused, then put a hand on his arm, not to help him up, which she perhaps sensed he would hate, but more likely to offer emotional support. "You got to me with what you said. There's a Starbucks just down the block, could you spare a little time and listen to me?"

Petey's lips puckered. "I, ah, I don't think so. I'm bad company, even for myself."

"Please. I won't bury you with sad stories, but I think we share some of the same demons."

"All right, I guess, but just for a half hour."

They left together, and for weeks they sat beside each other. Petey told the group that Holly had moved in with him. "She seems to be comfortable with me," he said. She held his hand and nodded.

A few months after that Petey showed up on his own, and Holly never appeared again. When asked about her absence, Petey's usual neutral courtesy was replaced with short, testy one-word responses, like "she's fine," and "you'll have to ask her." I'd felt obliged to corner him.

"All right, what's going on with you and Holly?"

"Go pick on somebody else, George."

"You're my best prospect. Let's go have a parking lot discussion."

Once outside I resumed.

"Did Holly take off? Relapse?"

Petey hesitated. "Nah. She's still living at my place. But not with me."

"Hah?"

"It started off good. After a few days we got— close, and I only needed to wash one set of sheets. She seemed okay with my legs. But a couple months later she moved back to the spare bedroom and told me we weren't working out. She takes care of her own food and cooking."

"But she doesn't do anything with you or for you?"

"Nah. It's like I'm not there. And I think she's been stealing some stuff and pawning it."

My anger surged. The manipulative bitch was abusing a cripple's hospitality. "Tell her to get the hell out!"

"I did, but she just ignored me."

"Get the cops to throw her out."

"I wish. She claims I told her she could stay as long as she needed to, that she's a tenant. It would cost me several thousand to go through legal proceedings, and even then there's no guarantee. She's not mean, just withdrew into a cocoon."

"Jesus. Do you want me to talk to her?"

"Yell at her, you mean? She'd probably just say we'd assaulted her."

"I'm really sorry, Petey. Maybe she'll find someone else to victimize. You're not helpless. Make her life so miserable that she leaves. Go online, check out other guys with similar problems. She's less company than your bad-tempered cat was, get her out."

His expression softened and saddened. "You may be right. She's not much better than my surly cat. Maybe if she finds someone else, she'll leave. But I've been alone for a long time, George. There's no pleasure left in her company, but there's a twisted comfort in her presence."

"That's a hell of a compromise," I said. And then it struck me that maybe Holly was also paying her dues, willing to abandon our group friendships and live next to an alienated Petey to avoid the hazards of a shelter. "Let's hope she finds someone else."

The Blues

Victor Clevenger

in the last eight months
i've not written a poem longer than five lines
but hey   what's a few hundred days
of sitting & whistling the blues
with the birds outside this broken window

DEAD MAN

Robert Beveridge

There is not a fresh
horse left in the west,
and a messenger watched
his pay, and his job,
fall by the wayside
with the advent
of the Industrial
Revolution.

Three hundred miles
away, a trader
sits before his campfire,
smokes rabbit and pipe
at the same time.
His wife lies in Albuquerque,
dead for days
of consumption.

For want of a fresh
horse, he will not know

until he arrives

with the diamond ring

he bought her in Tucson.

SHOWING UP YOUR PERV'S RAINBOW TANKA

Gerard Sarnat

i. Be Here Now tanka

Pre-disgraced Woody
Allen quipped, "80 percent
of success is just
showing up" -- maybe more when
talk 'bout red-letter friendship.

ii. Poor Richard's Off-Color Almanac tanka

Dumpster Dick Diving
On Cloudy Blue Afternoon
Then Kicked To The Curb
By School Bullies – It Is All
About Showing Up, Coming.

Now Scary Downer To Earth Reciprocation

Gerard Sarnat

I soooo do want to write much kinder, be sweeter.

Fly a bit less cleverly ironic. And not too very quotidian.

But try for Sarnatzky to connect us much more with hearts

plus our bodies than gaudy minds. Will you remain interested in me?

Still perhaps love Gerard authentically as he sure loves you? Pray tell…

How Beautiful Summer Is

Mark Simpson

as long as the truce holds, heat looming
just over the mountains, east of the Cascade ridge.

Small birds in the birdbath, flutter
and hop, bees there, too, resting—even the dog
sleeps in the sun, dreaming

of the sun and the cool nights. She lifts
her head and sniffs—she knows
what's coming as well as we do, scent in the wind,
pain in the bones.

Then it's here for real.
Grass drier than crisp, dead brown, firs droop
brittle green, fruit drops from the fruit trees.

Not enough water for all of us as we sip
from our warm cup.

No one keeps time now. Everyone waits for the end,
summer dead in its tracks.

No shadows in the hollows we've made for ourselves,

deep enough for a grave, someone wants to say,

but doesn't.

MUSIC IN THE AIR

Mark J. Mitchell

It felt like his teeth
caught lost radio signals
at random—so
early Elvis battled late
Costello over a bed
of rusted horns jazzing
and rattling his skull.

But on rare, cool
blue evenings—when
the air was clear
and he sat very still—
one lonely violin
would distil a fugue
through his molars.

Then he could sleep
the sleep of the just.

A Big Cigar

William Doreski

After a tropical storm
the air tastes like downtown Havana.
I should light a big cigar
to honor Karl Marx and survival
of the least fit among us,

especially including myself.
But having stayed up all night
on tornado watch I'm too tired
to strike a match. The colors
of the landscape remain simple

as a page torn from a bible.
The mucky puddles in the road
look bottomless. Walking downtown
to read a newspaper and pretend
I'm still an honest citizen

I leave a spoor that lingers
from a week in Cuba wasted
on cutting cane to support

Castro's indifferent politics.
How simplified that distant self

appears now that tropical storms
have abraded familiar landscapes
to lie as flat as billionaires' lawns.
Havana's plain white houses
and the sweet tough crop of cane

linger in watercolors scrawled
at the time, my inept artistry
bruising my aged ego.
Maybe I'll buy a big cigar
for my first smoke in fifty years.

With a clatter of church bells
the town will turn out to watch me
cough and wheeze and choke myself
on an ember sparked so long ago
I can't remember its source.

Contributors

In order of appearance

Available from Laughing Ronin Press

Snout Chasing Tail - Joseph Fulkerson

Famous Long Ago - Howie Good

Ploieşti - Kevin Tosca

Valentina Mezcalito Blues - Catfish McDaris

Upcoming from Laughing Ronin Press

Absence & Other Poems - John D Robinson

Daily Worship - Aimee Nicole

We Live The Songs - Steve Zmijewski

www.ingramcontent.com/pod-product-compliance
Lightning Source LLC
Chambersburg PA
CBHW070649130626
46555CB00006B/2784